Jupiter

BY DANA MEACHEN RAU

Content Adviser: Dr. Stanley P. Jones, Assistant Director, Washington, D.C., Operations, NASA Classroom of the Future

Science Adviser: Terrence E. Young Jr., M.Ed., M.L.S., Jefferson Parish (La.) Public Schools

Reading Adviser: Dr. Linda D. Labbo, Department of Reading Education, College of Education, The University of Georgia

COMPASS POINT BOOKS

MINNEAPOLIS, MINNESOTA

For Charlie

Compass Point Books
3722 West 50th Street, #115
Minneapolis, MN 55410

Visit Compass Point Books on the Internet at *www.compasspointbooks.com*
or e-mail your request to *custserv@compasspointbooks.com*

Photographs ©: NASA, cover, 1, 3, 6–7, 8–9, 10–11, 12, 17 (all), 18–19, 21, 24–25; North Wind Picture Archives, 4–5; Hulton Getty/Archive Photos, 5 (bottom right); USGS, 20; NASA/JPL/Caltech, 14–15, 22–23; Astronomical Society of the Pacific, 24 (bottom left), Marilyn Moseley LaMantia/Graphicstock, 11 (top right), 26–27.

Editors: E. Russell Primm, Emily J. Dolbear, and Karen Commons
Photo Researchers: Svetlana Zhurkina and Jo Miller
Photo Selector: Karen Commons
Designer: The Design Lab
Illustrator: Graphicstock

Library of Congress Cataloging-in-Publication Data

Rau, Dana Meachen.
    Jupiter / by Dana Meachen Rau.
        p. cm. — (Our solar system)
    Includes bibliographical references and index.
    Summary: Describes the size, characteristics, and composition of the planet Jupiter.
    ISBN 0-7565-0198-9 (hardcover)
    1. Jupiter (Planet)—Juvenile literature. [1. Jupiter (Planet)] I. Title.
    QB661 .R38 2002
    523.45—dc21   2001004418

Table of Contents

Looking at Jupiter from Earth

Have you ever eaten a scoop of rainbow sherbet with a cherry on the top? The planet Jupiter looks a little like that. It looks like a round ball of many colors with a large red dot. But if your scoop of sherbet was as big as Jupiter, it would be almost 90,000 miles (145,000 kilometers) wide! Jupiter is the largest planet in the **solar system**. It was named after the Roman god who ruled over all the other gods.

The largest planet in our solar system ▶
was named after Jupiter, the king of
all Roman gods.

People have been looking at Jupiter for thousands of years. It is bright, like a star. It can be seen without a telescope. In 1610, an Italian **astronomer** named Galileo Galilei (1564–1642) used a telescope to get a

◄ Galileo used a telescope like these when he found Jupiter's four biggest moons.

closer look at Jupiter. He found four moons around the planet. He named them Io, Europa, Ganymede, and Callisto.

In July 1994, a piece of ice and rock called a comet crashed into Jupiter. It was named Shoemaker-Levy 9. This was the first time scientists saw two objects in space hit each other. Many people on Earth used their telescopes to watch. The Hubble Space Telescope, a large telescope in space, took pictures of the crash. This event told us a lot about the giant planet.

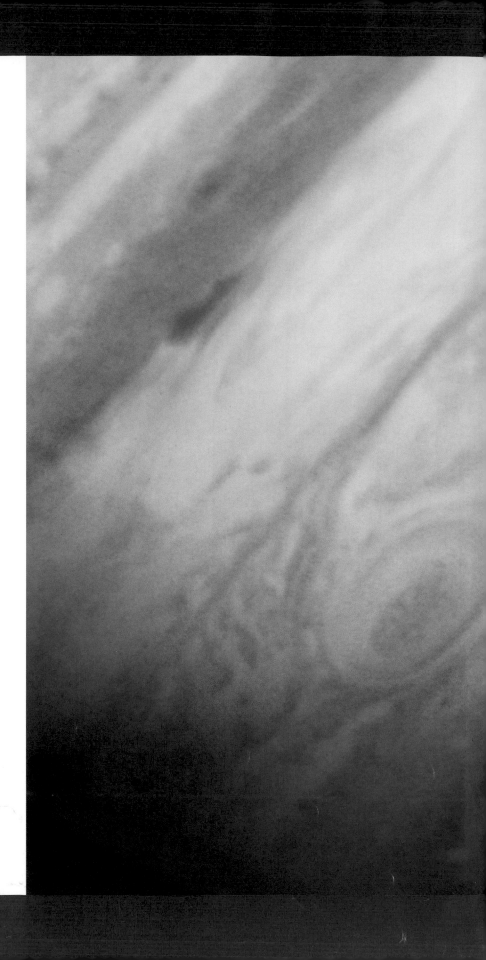

The Hubble Space Telescope took this picture of comet pieces crashing into Jupiter's atmosphere. ▶

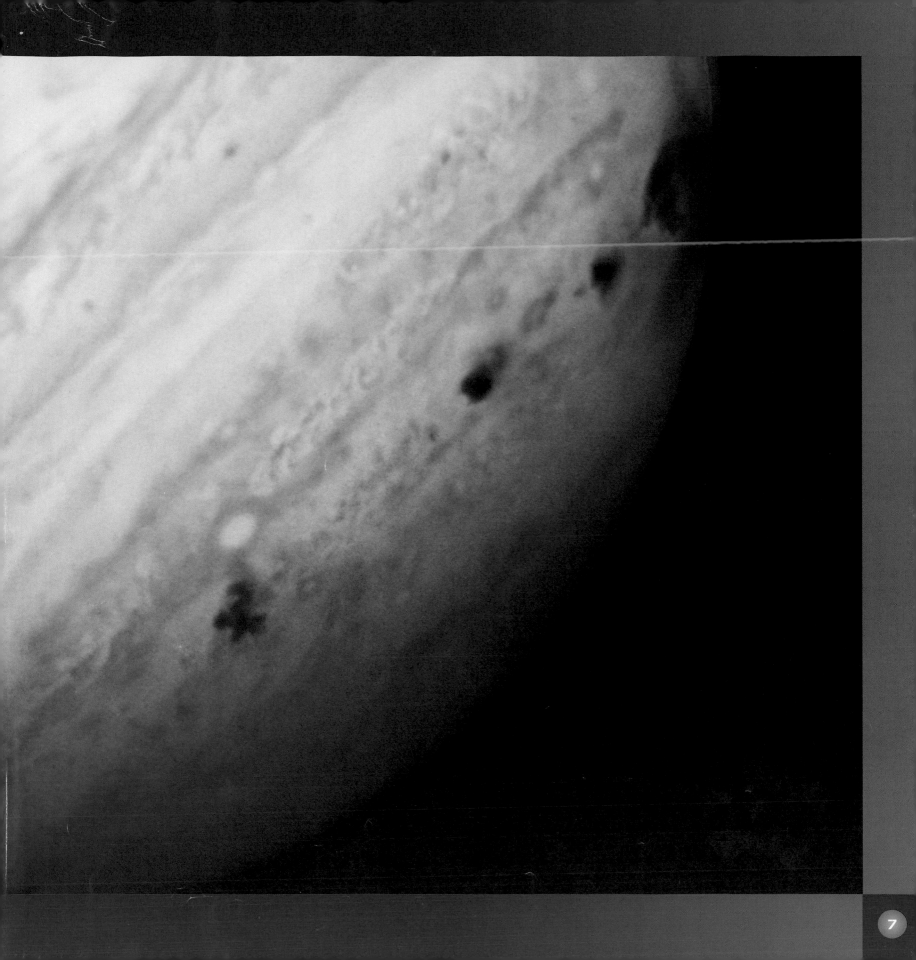

Looking at the Way Jupiter Moves

All planets spin, or rotate. One rotation is a planet's day. On Earth, our day is about 24 hours long. Jupiter has a very short day, however. It takes Jupiter less than 10 hours to spin around once.

While Jupiter rotates, it also revolves. Revolve means to travel around the Sun. Planets revolve along a path called an orbit. One trip around the Sun is a planet's year. It takes Jupiter a long time to orbit the Sun. One year on Jupiter is almost as long as twelve Earth years.

Jupiter and its moons take almost twelve ▶ *Earth years to circle the Sun once.*

Looking Through Jupiter

You could never visit Jupiter or stand on its surface. Jupiter is made mostly of gases, just like Saturn, Uranus, and Neptune. These planets are called gas giants. Jupiter does not have any solid ground like Earth does. Most of Jupiter is made of hydrogen gas.

Scientists believe that deep inside Jupiter may be a **core** of liquid or slushy rock or metal. The core might even be as hot as 36,000° Fahrenheit (20,000°

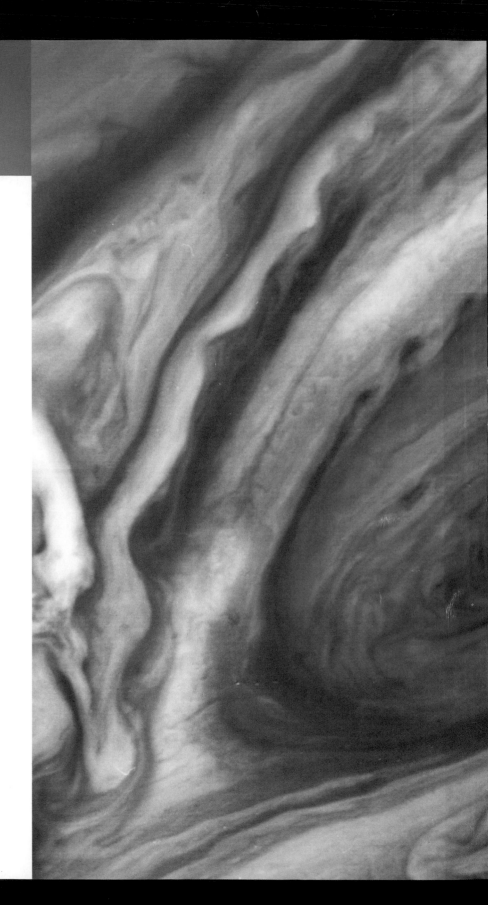

In 1979, Voyager 2 *took this picture as it ▶ flew past the Great Red Spot.*

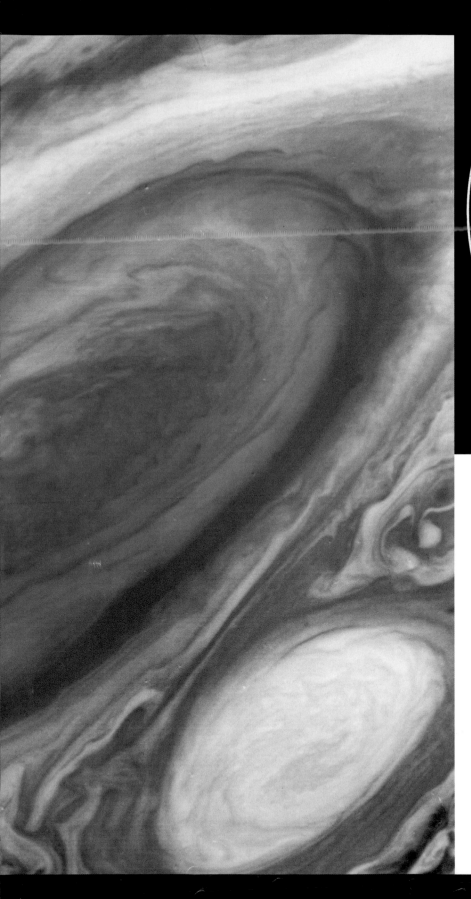

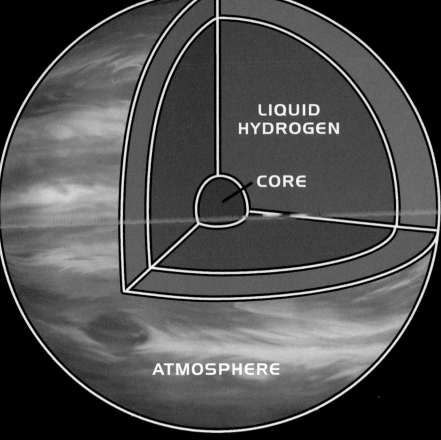

LIQUID
HYDROGEN

CORE

ATMOSPHERE

Celsius)! Layers of liquid hydrogen surround the core. Then comes Jupiter's atmosphere. A planet's atmosphere is made up of the gas and clouds around the planet.

The clouds in its atmos-

▲ *A cross-section illustration shows the layers of liquid hydrogen surrounding the planet's core.*

phere are one of the first things people notice about Jupiter. The clouds have colorful stripes called zones and belts. The zones are light in color. The belts are dark. The clouds have different colors because of their temperature and what they are made of. They also have different colors because of their **altitude**. Red clouds are the highest. Brown and white clouds make up the main layer. Blue clouds are the lowest in the atmosphere.

All the clouds move around Jupiter from east to west. High winds make them travel at speeds up to 400 miles (644 kilometers) per hour. The clouds create stormy weather on Jupiter. They are filled with lightning and powerful storms. The cloud patterns change all the time. Some change in just a few hours. Others change over many years.

One of the largest storms on Jupiter has been raging there for more than 300 years. This swirling storm is called the Great Red Spot. It is shaped like an oval. It is about 15,400 miles (24,800 kilometers) wide and 8,700 miles (14,000 kilometers) high. That's as big as two Earths side by side!

◄◄ *Jupiter's clouds have many colorful zones and belts. The large red oval at the lower right is the Great Red Spot.*

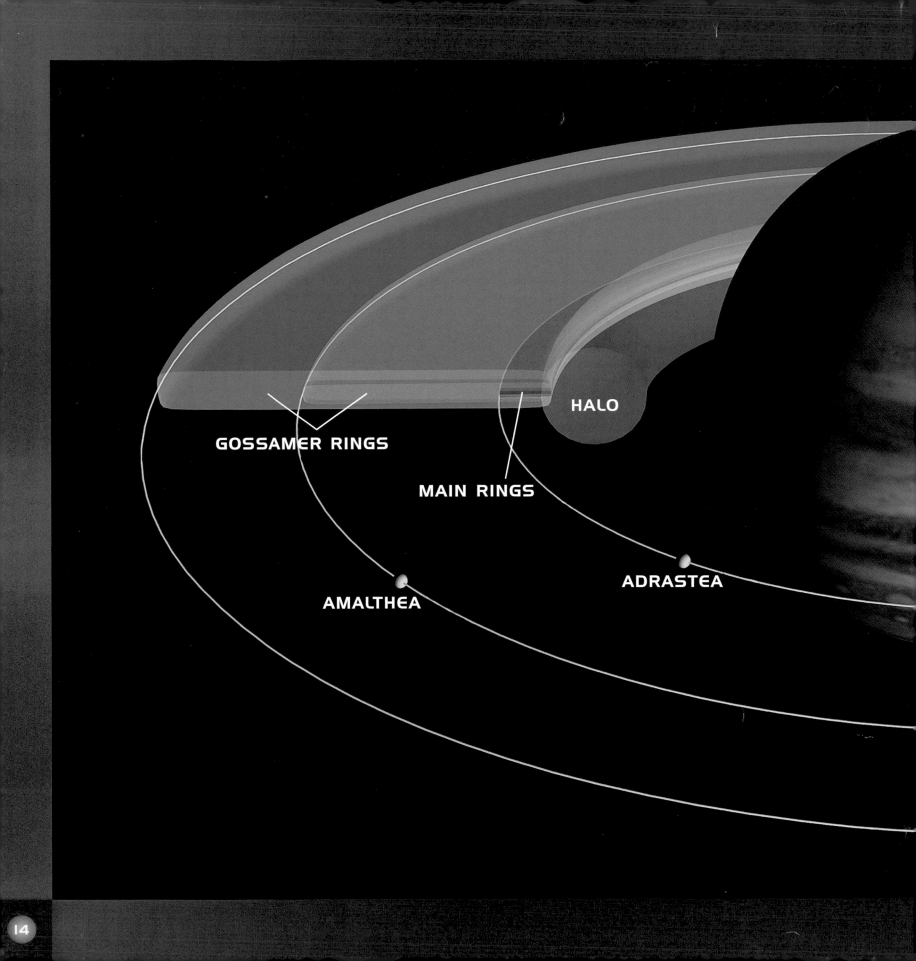

Looking Around Jupiter

✦ Most people know that Saturn has rings. They are icy and bright. In 1979, astronomers found that Jupiter has rings, too. Jupiter's rings are dark.

Jupiter has four rings around its middle. There are two faint outer rings, a flat main ring, and an inner cloudy ring. The rings are made mostly of tiny rocks and dust. This rock and dust was created when meteorites crashed into Jupiter's moons.

◀ *Jupiter has four rings and four small inner moons.*

METIS

THEBE

At least sixteen moons orbit around Jupiter. The planet has four large moons named Ganymede, Callisto, Europa, and Io. They are called the Galilean moons after Galileo. Astronomers study these moons very carefully. Ganymede is the largest moon in the solar system. It is covered with dark **craters** and light ridges. Callisto is covered with craters, too. It has an icy, rocky surface. Europa also has a layer of ice on its surface. Scientists think an ocean of liquid water or slushy ice may lie below Europa's surface. Io is much different than Europa. Io is bubbling and hot. It has the most active **volcanoes** in the solar system. The volcanoes shoot **lava** out more than 190 miles (300 kilometers) above the planet's surface.

Four smaller moons orbit close to Jupiter. Then come the four Galilean moons. Finally, there are at least eight outer moons. Four of these outer moons orbit in a direction opposite from the others.

An object that scientists think may be another moon also circles Jupiter. They call it S/1999 J1. But its orbit is very far from Jupiter. Scientists will watch it closely. Then they will decide if it can be called a moon.

Callisto (upper left), Europa (upper right), ▸▸
Io (lower left), and Ganymede (lower right)
are Jupiter's four biggest moons. They were
discovered by Galileo in 1610.

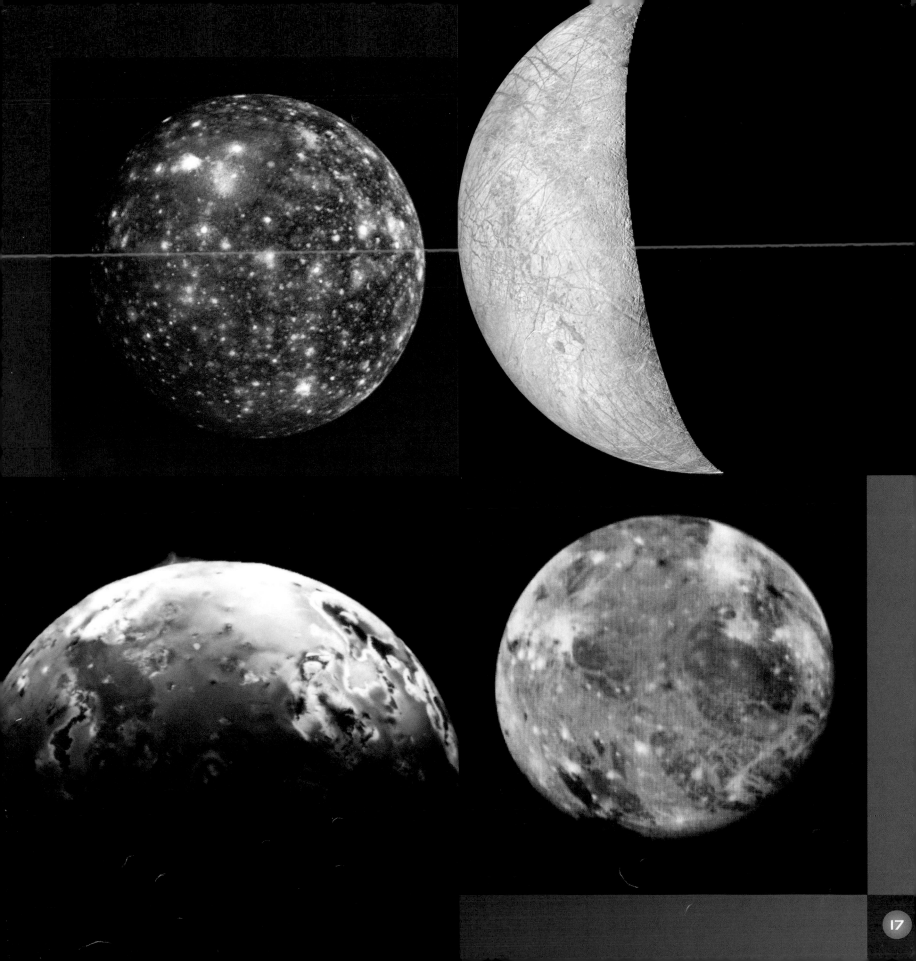

Looking at Jupiter from Space

⋆ Jupiter is one of the outer planets. The outer planets lie beyond a belt of **asteroids** that also orbit the Sun. The other outer planets are Saturn, Uranus, Neptune, and Pluto. It is hard to study Jupiter and the other outer planets by using telescopes because these planets are so far away from Earth. Many spacecraft have been sent to Jupiter to study it more closely.

Two very successful missions were sent to Jupiter in 1973 and 1974. The spacecraft were called *Pioneer 10* and

Pioneer 11. They sent back a lot of new information about Jupiter. After leaving Jupiter, *Pioneer 10* headed out of the solar system. *Pioneer 11* went on to study other outer planets.

In 1979, *Voyager 1* and *Voyager 2* flew by Jupiter. They discovered Jupiter's rings and some of its moons. Together, the two spacecraft took more than 33,000 pictures of Jupiter and its moons. They also saw storms and lightning in the clouds. They saw volcanoes shooting lava on Io as the spacecraft passed.

◀ Pioneer 11 *was launched on April 5, 1973, from Kennedy Space Center in Florida.*

Many spacecraft have flown by Jupiter. But one spacecraft, named *Galileo,* went into orbit around Jupiter. It could gather more information in orbit than in just flying by. In 1989, *Galileo* was released in space by the **space shuttle** *Atlantis.* It was the first spacecraft to orbit one of the outer planets. It went into orbit in 1995. It has been studying Jupiter ever since.

Galileo was made of two parts —an orbiter and a probe. The orbiter circled the planet. It is still

The Voyager spacecraft flew by ▲ Jupiter in 1979.

Galileo's orange, cone-shaped probe and ▸▸ 16-foot (5-meter)-wide orbiter were built at the Jet Propulsion Laboratory in California.

collecting information about Jupiter today. The probe dropped into the clouds of Jupiter's atmosphere in December 1995. It fell for almost an hour and sent back information about winds, temperatures, and clouds.

The next spacecraft to go to Jupiter will be the *Europa Orbiter* mission. It will be launched in 2008. It will look closely at Jupiter's moon Europa to see if an ocean of water lies beneath its frozen crust.

This illustration shows how NASA ▶
believes Europa Orbiter *will look when it reaches Jupiter in 2010.*

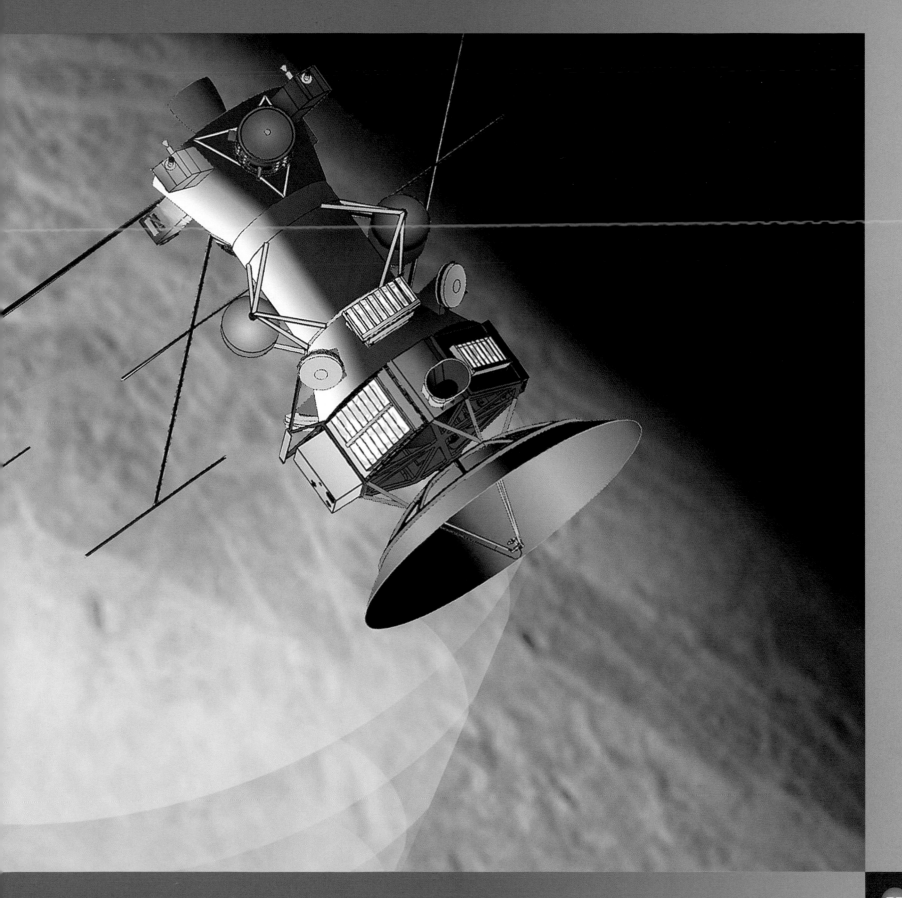

Looking to the Future

Astronomers still have many questions about Jupiter. They are very curious about the atmosphere. They want to know why the winds are so strong. And they want to know

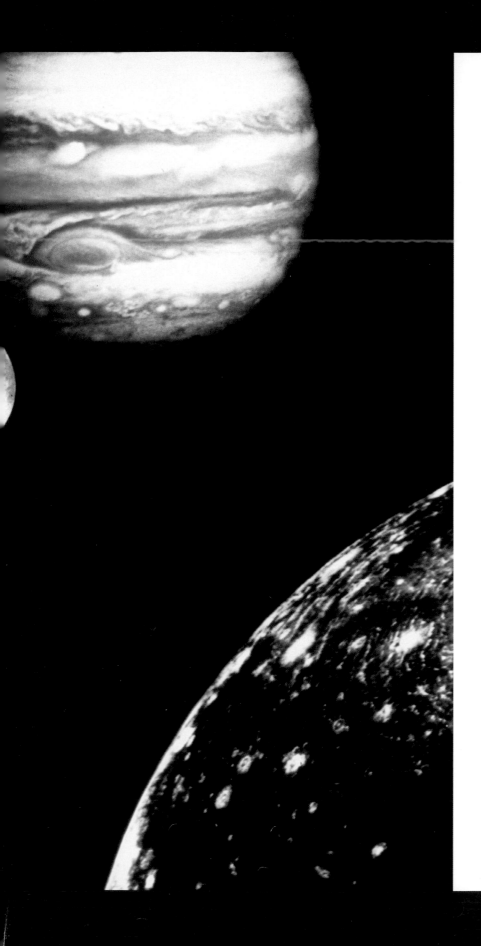

why the Great Red Spot has lasted so long.

Today, scientists are very interested in Europa. It might be the only other place in the solar system with a large amount of water, like Earth. Where there is water, there may be life, too. Scientists hope that *Europa Orbiter* will tell us if there is water (and maybe life) on this Jupiter moon.

◀◀ Scientists hope to learn why the stormy Great Red Spot has lasted so long.

◀ Scientists still have much more to learn about Jupiter and its moons.

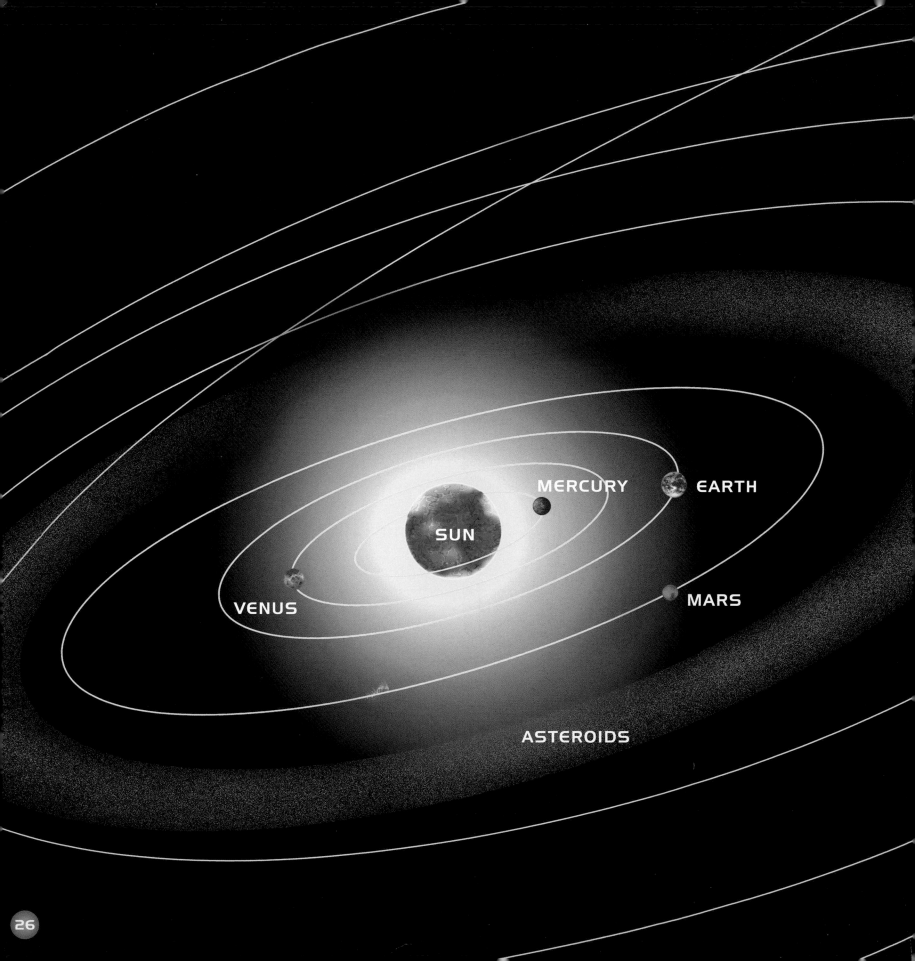

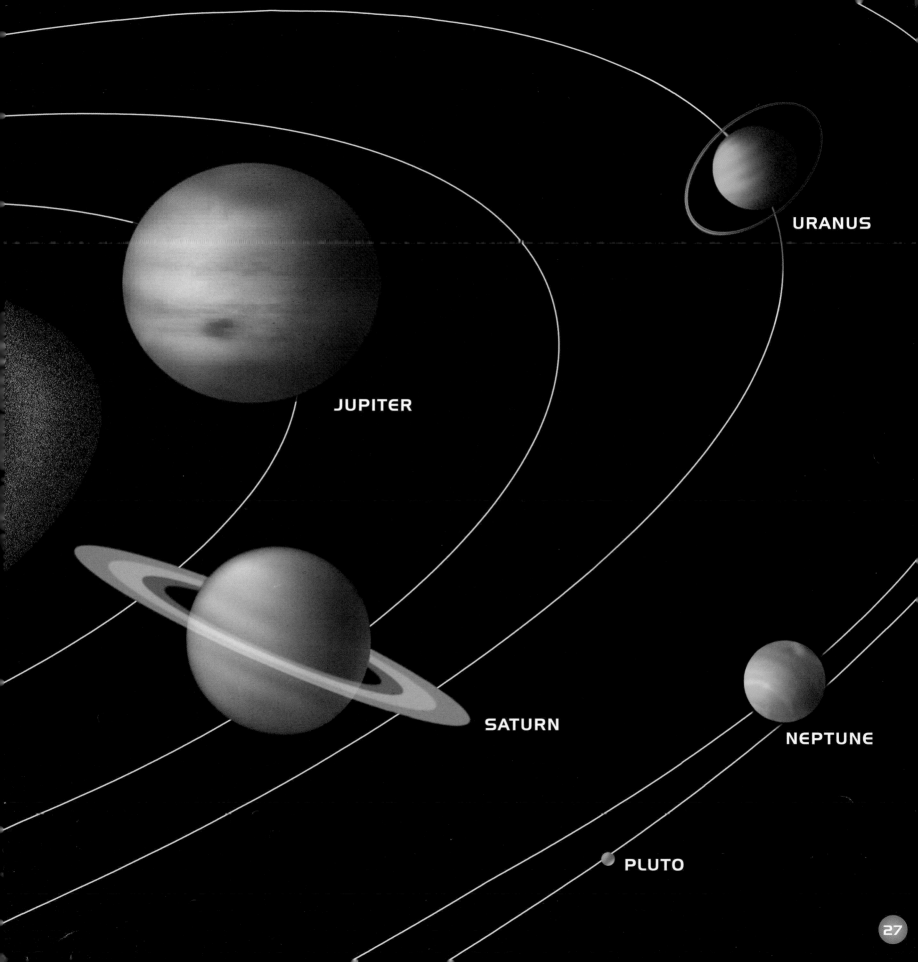

JUPITER

URANUS

SATURN

NEPTUNE

PLUTO

Glossary

altitude—height

asteroids—chunks of rock that orbit the Sun especially between the orbits of Mars and Jupiter

astronomer—someone who studies space

core—the center of a planet

craters—bowl-shaped landforms created by meteorites crashing into a planet

lava—liquid rock

meteorites—chunks of rock that hit a planet; when they travel in space before they land, they are called meteoroids

solar system—a group of objects in space including the Sun, planets, moons, asteroids, comets, and meteoroids

space shuttle—a spacecraft that carries astronauts who work in space and returns to Earth when its mission is complete

telescope—a tool astronomers use to make objects look closer

temperature—how hot or cold something is

volcanoes—mountains that may erupt with hot liquid rock

A Jupiter Flyby

Jupiter is the largest planet and the fifth planet from the Sun.

If you weighed 75 pounds (34 kilograms) on Earth, you would weigh 186 pounds (84 kilograms) on Jupiter.

Average distance from the Sun: 483 million miles (778 million kilometers)

Distance from Earth: 366 million miles (589 million kilometers) to 602 million miles (968 million kilometers)

Diameter: 88,846 miles (142,953 kilometers)

Number of times Earth would fit inside Jupiter: 1,300

Did You Know?

- Jupiter is larger than all the other planets combined.

- Some pieces of Jupiter's rings are so small that you would need a microscope to see them.

- Some people call Jupiter a "mini" solar system because it has so many moons.

- Jupiter's moon Ganymede is larger than the planets Pluto and Mercury.

- Some people say that Io looks like a pizza because it is yellow, white, and red, like bubbling cheese and pizza sauce.

- Io has so many volcanoes that lava covers almost its entire surface.

- Some important missions to Jupiter include *Pioneer 10, Pioneer 11, Voyager 1, Voyager 2,* and *Galileo.*

- *Pioneer 10* will travel through space until it reaches the closest star to the Sun— about 2 million years from now!

- Jupiter's moon Amalthea is constantly struck by meteorites that bury themselves in its surface and then explode.

- Jupiter is like a giant magnet. It can damage spacecraft that get too close.

Time it takes to orbit around Sun (one Jupiter year): 11.9 Earth-years

Time it takes to rotate (one Jupiter day): 9 hours and 55 minutes

Structure: core (liquid rock or metal), liquid hydrogen

Average temperature of cloud tops: −220° Fahrenheit (−140° Celsius)

Atmosphere: hydrogen, helium

Atmospheric pressure (Earth=1.0): 100

Moons: 16

Rings: 4

Want to Know More?

AT THE LIBRARY

Cole, Michael D. *Galileo Spacecraft: Mission to Jupiter.* Berkeley Heights, N.J.: Enslow Publishers, 1999.

Kerrod, Robin. *Jupiter.* Minneapolis: Lerner Publications, 2000.

Simon, Seymour. *Destination, Jupiter.* New York: Morrow Junior Books, 1998.

ON THE WEB

Exploring the Planets: Jupiter
http://www.nasm.edu/ceps/etp/jupiter/
For more information about Jupiter

Galileo Project Home
http://www.jpl.nasa.gov/galileo/
For more images, news, and other information about the *Galileo* mission, Jupiter, and its moons

The Nine Planets: Jupiter
http://www.seds.org/nineplanets/nineplanets/jupiter.html
For a multimedia tour of Jupiter

Solar System Exploration: Missions to Jupiter
http://sse.jpl.nasa.gov/missions/jup_missns/jup-cassini.html
For more information about important NASA missions to Jupiter

Space Kids
http://spacekids.hq.nasa.gov
NASA's space science site designed just for kids

Space.com
http://www.space.com
For the latest news about everything to do with space

Star Date Online: Jupiter
http://www.stardate.org/resources/ssguide/jupiter.html
For an overview of Jupiter and hints on where it can be seen in the sky

Welcome to the Planets: Jupiter
http://pds.jpl.nasa.gov/planets/choices/jupiter1.htm
For pictures and information about Jupiter and some of its most important surface features

THROUGH THE MAIL

Goddard Space Flight Center
Code 130, Public Affairs Office
Greenbelt, MD 20771
To learn more about space exploration

Jet Propulsion Laboratory
4800 Oak Grove Drive
Pasadena, CA 91109
To learn more about the *Galileo*
spacecraft and other missions to Jupiter

Lunar and Planetary Institute
3600 Bay Area Boulevard
Houston, TX 77058
To learn more about Jupiter and other
planets

Space Science Division
NASA Ames Research Center
Moffet Field, CA 94035
To learn more about Jupiter and
solar system exploration

ON THE ROAD

**Adler Planetarium and
Astronomy Museum**
1300 S. Lake Shore Drive
Chicago, IL 60605-2403
312/922-STAR
To visit the oldest planetarium
in the Western Hemisphere

***Exploring the Planets* and
*Where Next Columbus?***
National Air and Space Museum
7th and Independence Avenue, S.W.
Washington, DC 20560
202/357-2700
To learn more about the solar system
at this museum exhibit

**Rose Center for Earth and
Space/Hayden Planetarium**
Central Park West at 79th Street
New York, NY 10024-5192
212/769-5100
To visit this new planetarium and
learn more about the planets

UCO/Lick Observatory
University of California
Santa Cruz, CA 95064
408/274-5061
To see the telescope that was used to
discover the first planets outside of
our solar system

Index

◄ **About the Author**: *Dana Meachen Rau loves to study space. Her office walls are covered with pictures of planets, astronauts, and spacecraft. She also likes to look up at the sky with her telescope and write poems about what she sees. Ms. Rau is the author of more than sixty books for children, including nonfiction, biographies, storybooks, and early readers. She lives in Farmington, Connecticut, with her husband, Chris, and children, Charlie and Allison.*